U.S. History
Quick Starts

Author: Linda Armstrong
Editor: Mary Dieterich
Proofreaders: Margaret Brown and April Albert

COPYRIGHT © 2019 Mark Twain Media, Inc.

ISBN 978-1-62223-776-0

Printing No. CD-405042

Mark Twain Media, Inc., Publishers
Distributed by Carson-Dellosa Publishing LLC

Visit www.carsondellosa.com

Table of Contents

Introduction to the Teacher

To make informed decisions in today's complex world, students must understand our nation's history. Quality classroom instruction remains the cornerstone of any United States history program, but experienced educators know that learning requires effective reinforcement.

U.S. History Quick Starts offers teachers and parents short quick start activities to help students relate to important people, places, and events from our country's past. Used at the beginning of a social sciences time slot, these mini-tasks help students focus on understanding United States history.

The pages are grouped into units covering topics such as The Land and First People; Explorers and Colonizers; Revolutionaries and Pioneers; Slavery, Freedom, and Technology; and The United States as a World Power. Each page features two to four quick starts.

Some activities encourage creative thinking. These open-ended projects include student versions of period newspaper stories, faux pioneer diary entries, drawing conclusions about historical events, and short speeches supporting or opposing controversial issues.

Other activities require memory and critical-thinking skills. These tasks guide students to state cause-and-effect relationships between events, to compare and contrast characteristics or situations, or to list events in sequence.

Reproduce the pages and cut along the lines, then use each section as a ten-minute quick start to the day's lesson, or distribute copies of uncut pages so students can keep their completed exercises in a three-ring binder for reference. Some activities, particularly the creative tasks, will require another sheet of paper.

Either enlarged individual sections or uncut pages make excellent transparencies to share with the class.

The Land & First People

The Land & First People 1

Circle the names of rivers. (Names may continue in the next row.)

MISSISSIPPIREOHIOSPMISS

OURIMECOLORADOCOLUMBIA

RIOGRANDESACRAMENTOPO

TOMACSTHUDSON

STLAWRENCESNAKEYUKONDID

The Land & First People 2

In Utah, Arizona, New Mexico, and Western Colorado, flatlands can be a mile high. Circle the name of this lofty geographic region.

Colorado Desert

Colorado Plateau

Great Plains

Mississippi Delta

The Land & First People 3

In Latin, *insula* means island and *pen* comes from a word root that means almost. Circle the name of the state that is a peninsula.

Oregon   Ohio

Florida   California

Arizona   New York

The Land & First People 4

Many states have volcanoes, but only one state is a chain of volcanoes. Which one is it?

Hawaii   Alaska

Washington   California

Oregon   Florida

The Land & First People

The Land & First People 5

Unscramble the name of an ancient mountain range in the eastern United States.

CNPLAIAPAHA TAOUNNSIM

_____

_____

The Land & First People 6

Some of the first Americans came from Asia to Alaska across a land bridge now flooded by the ocean. Circle the location of this land bridge. (Names may continue in the next row.)

ATLANTICOCEAN

CABBERINGSTRA

ITFOPACIFIC

OCEANFUNLA

KEMICHIGAN

The Land & First People 7

Circle the names of five Native American tribes of the Great Plains. (Names may continue in the next row.)

TABLECROWSIOUXPHONE

DANCEPAWNEEPEACE

CHAIRCHEYENNEOSAGEPIPE

The Land & First People 8

The Mohawk, Oneida, Onondaga, Cayuga, and Seneca tribes formed a confederacy. The Five Nations League solved arguments and decided when to go to war. Unscramble the name of the language they spoke.

QUORSOII

_____

The Land & First People

The Land & First People 9

Unscramble these geographical features.

CKYRO UAINMOSNT _____

TEAGR KELAS _____

EGATR LINPAS _____

NCTAATLI OANCE _____

FICCIPA EOCAN _____

IIIISPMPSSS ELADT _____

The Land & First People 10

Circle the method Plains tribes used to send secret messages to friends across long distances.

     cell phones

sign language

smoke signals

     stone tablets

The Land & First People 11

Why did Native American tribes invent hand signals?

_____

_____

_____

_____

_____

_____

_____

The Land & First People

The Land & First People 12

Circle the names of six types of Native American homes. (Words may continue in the next row.)

PUEBLOBUFFALOWICKIUP

RIVERTEPEELONG

HOUSEHOGANOAKWIGWAM

The Land & First People 13

Unscramble four Native American uses for buffalo.

ODFO _____

HLRSTEE _____

THNGCLIO _____

ELFU _____

The Land & First People 14

Many Native Americans object to the celebration of Columbus Day. Why?

_____

_____

_____

_____

_____

_____

The Land & First People 15

Unscramble the names of six Native American leaders.

TEALETS _____

STCHUMEE _____

CCHSEOI _____

IMORENOG _____

TNSITIG BLUL _____

ZRYCA OREHS _____

The Land & First People

The Land & First People 16

Circle and write the names of two famous Native American women. (Words may continue in the next row.)

PRINTERCJLOSPOCAHON

TASDIANETERE

SASACAGAWEARRAELOOU

_____

_____

The Land & First People 17

Draw a line from each raw material to its corresponding Native American product.

mud   fringed dresses

grass   baskets

fur   pots

deerskin   warm robes

The Land & First People 18

Unscramble the names of four animals Native Americans hunted.

FAOUFLB _____

REDE _____

SSLEA _____

ABER _____

The Land & First People 19

Archaeologists have found macaw feathers and paintings of parrots in Anasazi ruins. From where might they have come? Circle the source. (Names may continue in the next row.)

FRANCEINDIACHINAGERMANY

CENTRALMEXICOGREATBRITAIN

The Land & First People

The Land & First People 20

Obsidian is a sharp, glassy rock created in volcanoes. Circle three things Native Americans made out of obsidian. (Words may continue in the next row.)

TELEVISONSARROW

HEADSHOUSESPEARPO

INTSBASKETSKNIVES

The Land & First People 21

Native American tribes of California ground acorns to make bread. Circle the kind of tree that was a common source near their homes.

pine   oak   cottonwood
fir   birch

How did Native Americans grind seeds and grains?

_____

_____

_____

The Land & First People 22

Why did Native American farmers of the Northeast sometimes plant dead fish with their corn and squash seeds?

_____

_____

_____

_____

_____

The Land & First People 23

Name some things a coastal group of Native Americans could trade with an inland group.

_____

_____

_____

_____

The Land & First People

The Land & First People 24

Why did Native Americans of the Great Plains live in tepees instead of wooden houses?

_____

_____

_____

_____

The Land & First People 25

Unscramble five foods eaten by Native Americans of the Northeast.

ESTSHNUTC _____

BIEERTRARSWS _____

LWID ICRE _____

FSHI _____

URETYK _____

The Land & First People 26

Circle three sentences that are true.

Native American tribes traded seeds with each other.

Native American tribes never traded seeds with each other.

Native American tribes stored seeds from year to year.

Native American women cared for the crops.

Native American children never worked outdoors.

The Land & First People

The Land & First People 27

Name a possible Native American use for seashells.

_____

_____

_____

_____

_____

_____

The Land & First People 28

Circle the names of five foods that were first cultivated by Native Americans and later spread around the world. (Words may continue in the next row.)

ICECREAMSWEETPOTATO

CORNSODASQUA

SHTOMATOPUMPKIN

ROASTBEEF

The Land & First People 29

Why did European diseases that were brought to America kill more Native Americans than Europeans?

_____

_____

_____

_____

_____

The Land & First People 30

Unscramble the mixed-up word in each sentence.

Sequoyah invented writing for the

HECEOKER language.

_____

Each symbol in Sequoyah's system

stood for a LSABYLEL.

_____

The Land & First People

The Land & First People 31

Native Americans often decorated pots and baskets with symmetrical designs. Shade in squares to make this design symmetrical.

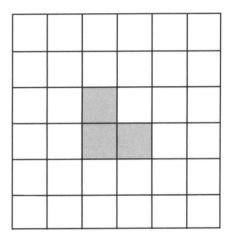

The Land & First People 32

In which region of the country would Native Americans use walrus tusks to make jewelry and fish hooks? Circle the answer.

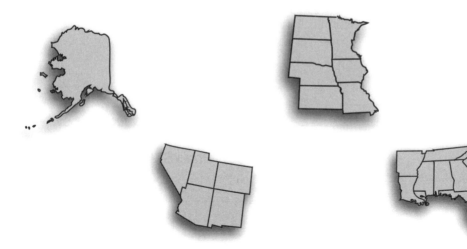

The Land & First People

The Land & First People 33

What did Native Americans use to carry and store water?

_____

_____

Name two water sources for Native Americans.

_____

_____

The Land & First People 34

Native Americans were often given names because of something that happened to them or something they did. Imagine you are called Red-in-the-Face. Explain how you got your name.

_____

_____

_____

_____

_____

The Land & First People 35

You are a Native American standing on a beach watching a European ship arrive. On another sheet of paper, tell what you see, how you feel, what you hope, and what you do.

The Land & First People 36

Southwestern tribes created sand paintings for use in ceremonies. On another sheet of paper, explain the value of a work of art that lasts only a few hours or a few days.

The Land & First People

The Land & First People 37

How might Native American life in the Northeast be the same as Native American life in the Pacific Northwest?

_____

_____

_____

_____

The Land & First People 38

How might Native American life in Alaska be different from Native American life along the coast of California?

_____

_____

_____

_____

The Land & First People 39

How might Native American life in Florida be different from life in a southwestern pueblo?

_____

_____

_____

_____

The Land & First People 40

How is your life the same as the life of a Native American child on the Plains? How is it different? Write your answer on another sheet of paper.

Explorers & Colonizers

Explorers & Colonizers 1

Explorers from Norway visited the North American continent shortly after the year 1000.

Unscramble the name these Norsemen gave the land.
NNLDVIA _____

Unscramble the name of a famous Norse explorer.
IFLE ORICNES _____

Unscramble this word. It means "a Norse legend."
GAAS _____

Explorers & Colonizers 2

Unscramble items European explorers traded for Asian luxuries.

LSEDAT RINGHER _____ _____

WOLO _____   ILO _____

UFSR _____   KNSIS _____

LSTA _____   RTA _____

Explorers & Colonizers 3

Draw a line from each sailing vessel to the country that used it.

caravel	Spain
junk	Polynesia
dhow	China
canoe	Portugal
galleon	Arabia

Explorers & Colonizers

Explorers & Colonizers 4

Circle the group of deepwater sailors and explorers who colonized the islands of the Pacific, including Hawaii, before the year 1000. (Names may continue in the next row.)

HAWAIIPOLYNESIANSALASKA

CHRISTOPHERCOLUMBUSVAS

CODAGAMAOAHUKA

WAIIAARTYCB

Explorers & Colonizers 5

In 1295, a merchant returned from a trip to the Far East and, while in jail, dictated his adventures to a writer. As a result, Europeans realized there was a great civilization in China. Unscramble this storyteller's name.

ORCMA LOOP

_____

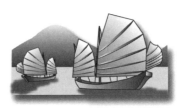

Explorers & Colonizers 6

Trade developed between Europe and Asia. Circle the items fourteenth century Europeans wanted from Asia. (Words may continue in the next row.)

ELECTRONICSSILKDISEASE

NUTMEGCOAL

CINNAMONPEPPER

WOODJEWELSWOOL

Explorers & Colonizers 7

Traders on the overland Silk Route between Europe and Asia kept raising prices. How did Europeans plan to get Asian goods for less?

_____

_____

_____

_____

_____

_____

Explorers & Colonizers

Explorers & Colonizers 8

Circle the names of Italian merchant cities that bought luxury goods from Arab traders and sold them to other Europeans. (Names may continue in the next row.)

NEWYORKVENICEENG

LANDPARISGENOA

LONDONLOSANGE

LESFLORENCENORWAY

Explorers & Colonizers 9

Unscramble the answers.

What European leader pioneered ship design and navigation?

CERPNI RHYEN HET AVIONGATR

_____

What country did he rule?

OARTUGPL _____

Around which continent did his ships sail?

RIACAF _____

Explorers & Colonizers 10

Special instruments helped sailors stay on course when land was out of sight. Unscramble the names of these instruments.

TRAOLABES _____

UATDNARQ _____

MPOSASC _____

Explorers & Colonizers 11

In 1498, a European explorer sailed around the Cape of Good Hope into the Indian Ocean and then continued to the port of Calcutta in India. Circle his name. (Names may continue in the next row.)

BALBOACHRISTOPHERCOL

UMBUSVASCODAGAMA

HERNANDOCORTEZBAR

TOLOMEUDIASSIRWRALEIGH

Explorers & Colonizers

Explorers & Colonizers 12

European explorers called the people they found in the Americas "Indians." Why?

_____

_____

_____

_____

_____

Explorers & Colonizers 13

Circle the name of the group of islands where Columbus landed.

Newfoundland

Hawaii

Bahamas

New Zealand

Explorers & Colonizers 14

A Spaniard leading a group of soldiers across the Isthmus of Panama in search of gold became the first European to see the Pacific Ocean. Unscramble his name.

OSVAC ZÑENU ED OLBABA

_____

Explorers & Colonizers 15

Christopher Columbus was Italian. Why didn't he claim his discovery for Italy?

_____

_____

_____

_____

_____

_____

Explorers & Colonizers

Explorers & Colonizers 16

Match each explorer or group to a famous ship.

Pilgrims   Santa Maria

Henry Hudson   Mayflower

Christopher   Half Moon
Columbus

Explorers & Colonizers 17

Sir Walter Raleigh tried to start a town twice in the same place. The second time, all of the colonists disappeared. Unscramble the name of Raleigh's ill-fated village.

KROOEAN _____

Circle the mysterious word that was carved on a tree. (Names may continue in the next row.)

MANHATTANVIRGINIADARE
CROATOANAZTECGOHOME
RALEIGHDISCOVERY

Explorers & Colonizers 18

Circle the name of the first successful British settlement in the New World.

Plymouth Plantation

Boston

Jamestown

New York

Explorers & Colonizers 19

Match each leader to his settlement.

Roger Williams   Plymouth
                       Plantation

William Penn   Jamestown

William Bradford   Rhode Island

John Smith   Pennsylvania

Explorers & Colonizers

Explorers & Colonizers 20

Match each person to what he was seeking in the New World.

Christopher Columbus	Gold and converts
Henry Hudson	The Fountain of Youth
Juan Ponce de León	A westward route to Asia
Robert Cavelier de La Salle	Tolerance and peace
William Penn	The Northwest Passage
Hernando Cortéz	Control of the fur trade

Explorers & Colonizers 21

Colonial children worked in the fields with their parents. Name three jobs that colonists had to do in order to raise a crop of corn.

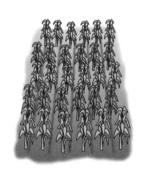

_____

_____

_____

_____

_____

Explorers & Colonizers 22

In addition to raising crops, New England colonists hunted and fished. Unscramble five items hunters or fishermen contributed to the family table.

TELORBSS _____

ELQSIRRUS _____

IBRASTB _____

ERDE _____

SLAMC _____

Explorers & Colonizers

Explorers & Colonizers 23

During colonial times, Town Criers roamed the streets ringing a bell and announcing the news. You are the Class Crier. What's the biggest class news event today?

Hear Ye! Hear Ye!

_____

_____

_____

_____

Explorers & Colonizers 24

Circle five toys children enjoyed in colonial days. (Words may continue in the next row.)

VIDEOSMARBLESCORN

HUSKDOLLSBALLS

KITESGOLFCLUBSSOC

CERICESKATES

Explorers & Colonizers 25

Unscramble the name of a tool that colonists used to change wool into yarn.

GIINPNNS WLEEH

_____

Explorers & Colonizers 26

Circle the name of the tool that colonists used to weave yarn into cloth.

V	M	M	Q
L	O	Q	B
Z	O	B	N
M	L	R	M

Explorers & Colonizers

Explorers & Colonizers 27

How did colonists use hornbooks?

_____

_____

_____

_____

_____

_____

Explorers & Colonizers 28

What was a trencher? Circle the answer.

a small shovel

a shared wooden plate

a narrow sled

a long ditch

Explorers & Colonizers 29

Circle three ways meat was stored in colonial times. (Words may continue in the next row.)

SMOKINGREFRIGERA

TINGSALTINGPICK

LINGBOXINGMIC

ROWAVING

Explorers & Colonizers 30

Why were harbors important to the Colonies?

_____

_____

_____

_____

_____

_____

_____

Explorers & Colonizers

Explorers & Colonizers 31

Match each colonial item to its source.

wool	grain
butter	sheep
house	animal fat
bread	trees
soap	cow's milk

Explorers & Colonizers 32

Why did the Southern Colonies have more slaves than the New England Colonies or the Middle Colonies?

_____

_____

_____

_____

_____

Explorers & Colonizers 33

Match each colonial craftsman to his product.

blacksmith	shoes
cobbler	leather
tanner	horseshoes
miller	barrels
cooper	flour

Explorers & Colonizers

Explorers & Colonizers 34

Native Americans taught New England colonists to make sugar from the sap  of a tree. We make candy and syrup from the same sap today. Circle the name of the tree. (Words may continue in the next row.)

OAKCOTTONWOODPINEAP

PLEMAPLESPRUCEELM

PALMBIRCHLARCHSYCAMORE

Explorers & Colonizers 35

How did British companies plan to make money from the colonies they sponsored?

_____

_____

_____

_____

_____

_____

Explorers & Colonizers 36

The oldest city in the United States was not built by British settlers. Circle its name.

Los Angeles

St. Augustine

Cincinnati

Santa Fe

Settlers from what nation built this city?

_____

Explorers & Colonizers 37

Indentured servants agreed to work five years to pay back the cost of their passage to America. You are an Irish teenager who has just agreed to become an indentured servant. On another sheet of paper, write a letter to your family explaining your decision.

Explorers & Colonizers

Explorers & Colonizers 38

During the French and Indian War, the British forced colonists to allow soldiers to sleep in their homes. You are a colonial teenager, and two British soldiers have been assigned to your house. On another sheet of paper, write a diary entry about your experience. What are your interactions with the soldiers? How does it make you and your family feel to have the soldiers there?

Explorers & Colonizers 39

To pay for the French and Indian War, the British charged taxes on more goods and services. Why were American colonists angry about these taxes?

_____

_____

_____

_____

Explorers & Colonizers 40

During the French and Indian War, many Native Americans joined forces with the French. You are a young Native American. Explain why your people are helping the French.

_____

_____

_____

_____

Revolutionaries & Pioneers

Revolutionaries & Pioneers 1

Circle the names of six colonies. (Names may continue in the next row.)

PENNSYLVANIAJEFFERSONNEW

YORKNORTHCAROLINA

FRANKLINNEWJERSEY

SOUTHCAROLI

NAOHIOGEORGIAIOWA

Revolutionaries & Pioneers 2

In 1763, the British proclaimed that all settlers had to leave the area between the Allegheny Mountains and the Mississippi River. Circle the reason.

to punish the colonists

to prevent problems with Native Americans

to prevent the spread of disease

to prepare the land for sale

Revolutionaries & Pioneers 3

Your parents are pioneers. A few years ago, they left Pennsylvania to build a cabin in the Ohio Valley. On another sheet of paper, write a diary entry about the British order to leave the valley and your parents' reaction.

Revolutionaries & Pioneers 4

In 1775, a hunter led a group of men into the Appalachians. They built a path to Kentucky called the Wilderness Road. Unscramble this famous trailblazer's name.

ALNIED OBOEN

_____

Revolutionaries & Pioneers

Revolutionaries & Pioneers 5

You are a member of the Massachusetts legislature. On another sheet of paper, write a short speech protesting British treatment of the Colonies.

Revolutionaries & Pioneers 6

On another sheet of paper, write a news story for the *London Daily*. Use this information:

Facts

Who: three groups of colonial rebels dressed as Native Americans
What: dump tea in harbor
When: evening of December 16, 1773
Where: Boston, Massachusetts Colony
Why: to protest the new tea tax

Revolutionaries & Pioneers 7

Your father is a cabinetmaker in London. Your family pays high taxes because of Britain's recent wars, and you have to wear outgrown shoes. How do you feel when you read the American colonists' complaints in the newspaper? Write your answer on another sheet of paper.

Revolutionaries & Pioneers 8

Circle the reason British troops marched to Lexington and Concord, Massachusetts, in April of 1775.

to kill all the Patriots

to seize Patriot supplies

to capture Paul Revere

to burn Ben Franklin's house

Revolutionaries & Pioneers

Revolutionaries & Pioneers 9

Unscramble the names of seven colonies.

IARGVNII _____   TAMCHUTASSSSE _____

RYLDMAAN _____   OEDRH ANISLD _____

ONUTCTICNEC _____   LDAEERAW _____

WNE EHPSAHMRI _____

Revolutionaries & Pioneers 10

Unscramble the name of the poet who wrote

"Paul Revere's Ride."

YNHER DSWOATRWH LFELOLOWNG

_____

Write the opening words of that poem in order.

"ride and Revere of the children my hear listen shall of midnight Paul you."

_____

_____

Revolutionaries & Pioneers 11

Who were the Minutemen, and how did they get their name?

_____

_____

_____

_____

Revolutionaries & Pioneers

Revolutionaries & Pioneers 12

Several riders warned Patriots that British troops were headed toward Lexington. Why do most people remember only one messenger?

_____

_____

_____

_____

_____

_____

Revolutionaries & Pioneers 13

Benjamin Franklin was a writer, printer, and inventor, as well as a Patriot. One of his sayings was "Make haste slowly." On another sheet of paper, give an example of what happens if you don't follow his wise advice.

Revolutionaries & Pioneers 14

Circle the qualities that made Benjamin Franklin valuable to the Patriot cause.

charm

marksmanship

battle strategies

intelligence

physical strength

wit

Revolutionaries & Pioneers 15

When the Stars and Stripes first became the country's official flag, how many stars did it have?

_____

What did they represent?

_____

How many stars are on the flag today?

_____

Revolutionaries & Pioneers

Revolutionaries & Pioneers 16

Draw lines matching Revolutionary places and events.

Yorktown	Patriot victory in 1777
Philadelphia	A hard winter for Patriots
Saratoga	British surrender
Lexington	"The shot heard 'round the world"
Boston	A "tea party"
Valley Forge	Declaration of Independence approved

Revolutionaries & Pioneers 17

Draw lines matching men and contributions.

Thomas Jefferson	author of *Common Sense*
George Washington	trained Patriot troops
Thomas Paine	commanded Patriot forces
Friedrich von Steuben	rode to warn Patriots
Paul Revere	author of Declaration of Independence

Revolutionaries & Pioneers 18

Draw lines matching women and their contributions during the Revolution and early years of the United States.

Margaret Corbin	fought in the war disguised as a man
Sacagawea	fought in the war in place of her fallen husband
Dolley Madison	wrote political poetry, commentary, and history
Deborah Sampson	saved national treasures from the burning White House
Mercy Otis Warren	guided Lewis and Clark

Revolutionaries & Pioneers

Revolutionaries & Pioneers 19

Your father has chosen to join General Washington's army. On another sheet of paper, write your father a letter expressing your feelings.

Revolutionaries & Pioneers 20

Number the four Revolutionary events in order.

_____ Approval of Declaration of Independence

_____ Boston Massacre

_____ Surrender at Yorktown

_____ French fleet arrives

Revolutionaries & Pioneers 21

In 1775, Ethan Allen and his Green Mountain Boys boosted Patriot morale by capturing a British fort on Lake Champlain. Unscramble the name of the fort.

TORF NROGTAIDECO

_____

Revolutionaries & Pioneers 22

Loyalists were colonists who did not support the Patriot cause. They remained loyal British citizens. Your parents are Loyalists. On another sheet of paper, explain your family's position to a friend whose parents are Patriots.

Revolutionaries & Pioneers

Revolutionaries & Pioneers 23

In 1775, the British defeated Patriot forces near Boston, Massachusetts. Circle the name of that battle. (Words may continue in the next row.)

PATRIOTSTORIESTHEBATTLE

OFBUNKERHILLCONTINENTAL

SOLDIERSINFANTRY

Revolutionaries & Pioneers 24

After the British surrendered, the United States continued to be governed by the Articles of Confederation. Soon it became clear that changes would have to be made. Representatives of the states designed a lasting government for our new nation. Unscramble the name of the gathering that accomplished this important work.

TUNCTONSTIALIO VEIONTCONN

_____

Revolutionaries & Pioneers 25

Delegates decided to separate the new government into three parts. Circle those three parts. (Words may continue in the next row.)

JUDICIALBRANCHHSTREEXECU

TIVEBRANCHLLCELEGISLATIV

EBRANCHDEWQOOE

Revolutionaries & Pioneers 26

The "Preamble," or introduction, to the Constitution begins with the words, "We the People." It goes on to say that the people are creating their own government. You are the king or queen of a European country. On another sheet of paper, tell what you think of this revolutionary idea.

Revolutionaries & Pioneers

Revolutionaries & Pioneers 27

Unscramble two of six important goals listed in the Preamble to the Constitution.

OT FRMO A OERM CERFPET UONNI _____

_____

OT LISEBSTAH TISECJU _____

_____

Bonus: Name another goal from the Preamble.

_____

Revolutionaries & Pioneers 28

Club constitutions set up guidelines for choosing leaders, getting supplies, and holding meetings. Write one item to include in a new science fiction club constitution.

_____

_____

_____

_____

Revolutionaries & Pioneers 29

Soon after the states ratified the Constitution, representatives approved ten important additions.

What do we call these amendments?

_____

Which of these ten ammendments do you think is the most important?

_____

Revolutionaries & Pioneers

Revolutionaries & Pioneers 30

The first amendment says the government cannot take away freedom of speech. Does that mean people can say anything they want? Write a paragraph on another sheet of paper giving an example of speech the Constitution might not protect.

Revolutionaries & Pioneers 31

Circle the group or groups qualified to vote in America's first elections.

African slaves

white women

men who owned land

white men without land

Revolutionaries & Pioneers 32

One U.S. city isn't part of any state. Unscramble its name.

GTWASCHINOND

_____

Why isn't it in a state?

_____

_____

_____

Revolutionaries & Pioneers 33

In 1803, President Jefferson bought some land from France. Unscramble the name of this fifteen-million-dollar real estate deal.

HET ANSALOIUI UEPHRCAS

_____

Revolutionaries & Pioneers

Revolutionaries & Pioneers 34

In 1804, Jefferson sent an expedition out to explore the country's new territory. Circle the leaders of this expedition. Write their names on the lines. (Names may continue in the next row.)

CCLOIMUYGFREWAMERIWETH

ERLEWISOOPSWRRYXZWI

LLIAMCLARKNNBVCURRQPL

_____

_____

Revolutionaries & Pioneers 35

In 1811, an important new service was launched on the Mississippi River. Unscramble it.

ATMTEOASB

_____

Revolutionaries & Pioneers 36

In 1800, the United States government moved from Philadelphia to Washington, D.C. Only fourteen years later, someone set fire to the new capital. Who did it? Circle the correct answer, and then explain what was happening at the time in the blanks below.

TERRORISTS   VANDALS   THE FRENCH   THE BRITISH

_____

_____

_____

Revolutionaries & Pioneers

Revolutionaries & Pioneers 37

On another sheet of paper, write a newspaper story about the building of the Erie Canal.

Facts

Who: Thousands of workers
What: a canal 363 miles long and four feet deep
When: July, 1817–October, 1825
Where: from the Hudson River to Lake Erie
Why: to carry passengers and cargo

Revolutionaries & Pioneers 38

You are a forty-niner with a bad case of gold fever. You can get to California's diggings on horseback, by wagon train, or on a ship that rounds Cape Horn. Make your choice and explain it. Use another sheet of paper.

Revolutionaries & Pioneers 39

It is your first night on the Oregon Trail. You are sitting beside the camp-fire. On another sheet of paper, write a diary entry about leaving something or someone behind.

Revolutionaries & Pioneers 40

You run a Chinese laundry in a California gold camp. List and explain the advantages and disadvantages of your job below.

Advantages _____

_____

_____

Disadvantages _____

_____

_____

Slavery, Freedom, & Technology

Slavery, Freedom, & Technology 1

It is 1860, and you live in St. Joseph, Missouri. Your brother has just signed up to be a rider for a special fast mail  service. Unscramble the name of his new employer.

HET PYON SRSEPXE

_____

Slavery, Freedom, & Technology 2

In 1861, telegraph wires reached from San Francisco to New York City. How were messages sent? Decipher the code and write each letter on the line below it.

_ _ _ _ _ .-. . . . . .

___ ___ ___ ___ ___

-.- - - - -.. .

___ ___ ___ ___

(**Hint:** . = e, - - - = o, - . . = d)

Slavery, Freedom, & Technology 3

In 1820, the North and South found a temporary solution to their problems with each other. Each side gave up something to keep the government in balance. Circle the name of their agreement. (Names may continue in the next row.)

CVBOPRESAXTHEMISSOURI

COMPROMISEMMBOPY

ESCRSPOINDIANA

TENNESSEEYR

Slavery, Freedom, & Technology 4

Unscramble the name of the boundary between Pennsylvania and Maryland that separated slave states from free states.

TEH ANSOM-XINOD INLE

_____

_____

Slavery, Freedom, & Technology

Slavery, Freedom, & Technology 5

A famous young enslaved woman escaped from her master in Maryland and found freedom in Pennsylvania. She returned to the South many times to help other slaves escape. Unscramble her name.

RIEHRAT BMTUAN

_____

Slavery, Freedom, & Technology 6

Eli Whitney's cotton gin helped cotton plantations make more money. Circle what the machine did.

planted cotton

picked cotton

removed cotton seeds

baled cotton

Slavery, Freedom, & Technology 7

Circle what happened as more and more planters used the cotton gin.

fewer slaves were needed
more slaves were needed
all slaves were freed
nothing changed

Explain your answer. _____

_____

_____

_____

Slavery, Freedom, & Technology 8

Circle the legal term used to describe slaves in the South. (Words may continue in the next row.)

CITIZENSPERSONS

PROPERTYHUMANS

PEOPLEGENTLEMENOWN

ERSVOTERSLEADERS

Slavery, Freedom, & Technology

Slavery, Freedom, & Technology 9

How did the settlement of new lands cause problems between Northern and Southern states?

_____

_____

_____

_____

_____

Slavery, Freedom, & Technology 10

Why was it against the law for slaves to learn to read?

_____

_____

_____

_____

_____

Slavery, Freedom, & Technology 11

Circle the names of six of the states that seceded from the Union at the time of the American Civil War, and then list them below. (Names may continue in the next row.)

ALABAMAMAINETEXASEAEBGEORGIANEWYORKV

MISSISSIPPIFLORIDALOUISIANATRYSEIURD

_____   _____

_____   _____

_____   _____

Slavery, Freedom, & Technology

Slavery, Freedom, & Technology 12

Unscramble the name of the first state to secede from the Union.

HOUST RONALCAI

_____

Slavery, Freedom, & Technology 13

Unscramble the name of the nation the Southern states created in 1861.

HET RCOEEATNFED

ATSTES FO EAAICMR

_____

_____

Slavery, Freedom, & Technology 14

At the beginning of the Civil War, the North had six times as many textile factories as the South. Why did this give the North an advantage?

_____

_____

_____

_____

Slavery, Freedom, & Technology 15

For what did the South hope when the Civil War began? Underline all correct answers.

The Union wouldn't fight.

The Union would give up.

England or France would help the South.

The North would run out of supplies.

Slavery, Freedom, & Technology

Slavery, Freedom, & Technology 16

Unscramble the names of the last states to secede from the Union.

RGINVIIA

_____

SAASKRAN

_____

ESETSENEN

_____

ORNHT RANIALOC

_____

Slavery, Freedom, & Technology 17

Circle the federal fort the Confederates captured in the first engagement of the Civil War. (Names may continue in the next row.)

FORTMCHENRYFORTNASSAUD

FORTTOWNSENDFORTSUMTER

FORTPHANTOMHILLFORTORA

Slavery, Freedom, & Technology 18

Why did the North send ships to blockade Southern ports?

_____

_____

_____

_____

_____

Slavery, Freedom, & Technology 19

A bloody battle in 1863 was the turning point of the war. President Abraham Lincoln gave a speech to dedicate the cemetery. Unscramble the name of the battlefield.

EGTTBRGYSU

_____

Slavery, Freedom, & Technology

Slavery, Freedom, & Technology 20

Write the name of each general in the correct column.

Grant   Lee   Jackson   Sherman
Longstreet   Beauregard   Burnside   McClellan

Union	**Confederacy**
_____	_____
_____	_____
_____	_____
_____	_____

Slavery, Freedom, & Technology 21

Circle the name of the spot where the South surrendered, ending the Civil War. (Names may continue in the next row.)

GETTYSBURGCE

METERYAPPOMAT

TOXCOURTHOUSE

RICHMONDWASH

INGTONDC

Slavery, Freedom, & Technology 22

Which document freed some of the slaves during the Civil War?

_____

_____

Which amendment freed all the remaining slaves in the United States?

_____

_____

Slavery, Freedom, & Technology

Slavery, Freedom, & Technology 23

If "transatlantic" means "across the Atlantic," what does "transcontinental" mean? Write another word that contains the root "trans."

_____

_____

_____

_____

_____

Slavery, Freedom, & Technology 24

By 1860, there were many railroad lines in the eastern part of the country. Why did the United States need a transcontinental railroad?

_____

_____

_____

_____

_____

_____

Slavery, Freedom, & Technology 25

In 1862, two railroad companies began laying transcontinental track. Draw a line matching each company to its starting place and the direction it was heading.

Union Pacific   Omaha, west

Central Pacific   Sacramento, east

Slavery, Freedom, & Technology 26

Unscramble the letters to name a kind of insect that sometimes swarmed across the prairie, eating all of the homesteaders' crops.

SASHGPEROPRS

_____

Slavery, Freedom, & Technology

Slavery, Freedom, & Technology 27

Circle the name of a book about life on the Great Plains. (Titles may continue in the next row.)

SOUNDERLITTLEHOUSE

ONTHEPRAIRIEHARRY

POTTERTHESECRET

GARDENMARY

Slavery, Freedom, & Technology 28

On the lines, write one advantage and one disadvantage of being a pioneer on the Great Plains.

advantage: _____

_____

_____

disadvantage: _____

_____

_____

Slavery, Freedom, & Technology 29

Your father is chief of a Great Plains tribe. On another sheet of paper, write a letter to the American president about what is happening to your people during the last half of the nineteenth century.

Some Plains tribes: Arapaho, Cheyenne, Comanche, Crow, Kiowa, Pawnee, and Shoshone

Slavery, Freedom, & Technology 30

For each item below, write *PT* for Plains Tribes or *H* for Homesteaders.

_____ lived in groups

_____ lived as single families

_____ lived in sod houses

_____ planted corn

_____ hunted buffalo (bison)

_____ lived in tepees

Slavery, Freedom, & Technology

Slavery, Freedom, & Technology 31

In 1876, several Native American tribes gathered to fight U.S. soldiers. A famous cavalry officer and all of his men were killed.

Unscramble the officer's name: ORGEGE RMONASTGR TUCSER

_____

Unscramble the name of the battlefield: LTETLI GBIONRH

_____

Unscramble the name of one of the Native American leaders: HICEF TNGISIT ULBL

_____

Slavery, Freedom, & Technology 32

On November 18, 1883, Congress established the time zones we use today. Before that, every city had its own time. Why did standard time become important after the transcontinental railroad was built? Write the answer on another sheet of paper.

Slavery, Freedom, & Technology 33

In 1874, Joseph Glidden invented a new kind of fencing called *barbed wire*. On another sheet of paper, answer the following questions:

Why was this fencing good for the farmers of the plains?

Why did cattlemen cut barbed wire fences?

Slavery, Freedom, & Technology

Slavery, Freedom, & Technology 34

On March 10, 1876, an immigrant from Scotland discovered a way to send voices through wires. Unscramble his name and the name of his invention.

EDLRXAEAN AGAMRH ELBL

_____

NEPHTELOE

_____

Slavery, Freedom, & Technology 35

Circle three things Thomas Alva Edison invented. (Words may continue in next line.)

WHEELPHONOGRAPHPAPER

CLIPMOTIONPICTUREMACH

INELIGHTBULBCOTTONGIN

Slavery, Freedom, & Technology 36

On another sheet of paper, write a newspaper story about a famous Chicago settlement house.

Facts
Who: Jane Addams and Ellen Gates Starr
What: open a settlement house, Hull House
When: September, 1889
Where: Chicago
Why: to help immigrant families adjust to life in America and provide recreational opportunities for children

Slavery, Freedom, & Technology 37

The first automobile was built in 1801, but it wasn't until the early 1900s that an American manufacturer found a way to produce practical cars ordinary people could afford. Unscramble his name and the manufacturing technique he developed.

NEYRH RFDO

_____

ALYSEMSB ILEN

_____

Slavery, Freedom, & Technology

Slavery, Freedom, & Technology 38

How would our lives be different without trucks or automobiles?

_____

_____

_____

_____

_____

Slavery, Freedom, & Technology 39

In 1903, two brothers tested an invention that would change the world. Unscramble their names and their high-flying contraption.

LURBWI NDA VRLEILO GTRIWH

_____

ANLIREAP

_____

Slavery, Freedom, & Technology 40

Number these events in order (1 being the earliest to 4 the most recent).

_____ Transcontinental Railroad completed

_____ Civil War ends

_____ First successful airplane flight

_____ Abraham Lincoln elected

The U.S. as a World Power

The U.S. as a World Power 1

Draw lines to match each industrialist to his industry.

William Astor   banking

J.P. Morgan   steel

John D. Rockefeller   oil

Andrew Carnegie   real estate

The U.S. as a World Power 2

Unscramble the name of a strategy workers developed to get fairer treatment in the workplace.

REISTK

_____

The U.S. as a World Power 3

Circle the names of three labor leaders. (Names may continue in the next row.)

COLGRNEUGENEDEBSDV

BEAMOTHERJONESOP

IUMMYTSAMUELGOMP

ERSUIRTINBCW

The U.S. as a World Power 4

Unscramble the full name of the labor union known as the "AFL."

ARNIECAM FARIOEDTEN

FO LORBA

_____

_____

The U.S. as a World Power

The U.S. as a World Power 5

In collective bargaining, who settles arguments between workers and employers? Underline the answer(s).

all workers and the employer

elected representatives and the employer

a panel of bosses

a panel of workers

The U.S. as a World Power 6

What were crowded, rundown city apartments called? Unscramble the answer.

NTNEEMTES

_____

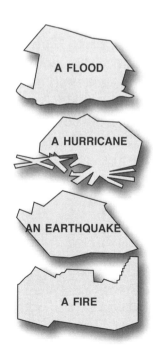

The U.S. as a World Power 7

Circle the disaster that destroyed downtown Chicago in 1871.

Draw a picture in the space below of who was blamed for the disaster.

A FLOOD

A HURRICANE

AN EARTHQUAKE

A FIRE

The U.S. as a World Power

The U.S. as a World Power 8

When a newspaper reporter and photographer named Jacob Riis made New Yorkers aware of the terrible conditions in their city's slums, many improvements were made. On your own paper, describe one problem you think reporters should write about today.

The U.S. as a World Power 9

Circle the name of the former slave who founded the Tuskegee Institute of Alabama. (Names may continue in the next row.)

THOMASJEFFERSONBOOKERT

WASHINGTONCSEOPIEN

JACOBRIISJPMORGAN

The U.S. as a World Power 10

When a play called "The Melting Pot" opened in 1908, thousands of immigrants were entering the United States. The play's title described the way cultural differences often melted away. Why do many people today disagree with the idea of a "melting pot"? Write your answer on another sheet of paper.

The U.S. as a World Power 11

A *monopoly* is a business that has no real competition. On another sheet of paper, explain how competition improves products, services, and pricing. Give an example.

The U.S. as a World Power

The U.S. as a World Power 12

When the people of Cuba revolted against Spanish rule in 1898, the United States sent a ship to Havana to protect American interests. This ship was named after a state. Unscramble its name.

EIMAN _____

What happened to the ship? _____

_____

_____

The U.S. as a World Power 13

Circle the answer to this question:

What made many ordinary Americans call for war against Spain?

sugar shortages

newspaper articles

McKinley's fiery speeches

The U.S. as a World Power 14

Circle the names of three territories the U.S. received from Spain at the end of the Spanish-American War. (Names may continue in the next row.)

VALENCIAPHILIPPINEISLANDSMEXICOGU

AMPUERTORICOCALIFORNIAARIZONA

The U.S. as a World Power

The U.S. as a World Power 15

Unscramble the name of the volunteer cavalry unit Theodore Roosevelt helped to organize during the Spanish-American War.

OHUGR SRIRDE

_____

The U.S. as a World Power 16

How did Theodore Roosevelt become president? Circle the answer.

He was elected by a small margin.

He was elected by a landslide.

He was vice president when the president was shot.

The U.S. as a World Power 17

Draw a line from the president's name to the event that occurred during his presidency.

Theodore Roosevelt   The Great Depression

William McKinley   Spanish-American War

Herbert Hoover   World War I

Woodrow Wilson   Trust-busting

The U.S. as a World Power

The U.S. as a World Power 18

Number the following presidents in the order in which they served (1 being the earliest to 4 the latest):

_____ Woodrow Wilson

_____ Abraham Lincoln

_____ Theodore Roosevelt

_____ John F. Kennedy

The U.S. as a World Power 19

Four states entered the Union in 1889. Unscramble their names.

TOHNR KATAOD

_____

NANMOTA

_____

TUHSO TAKDOA

_____

ITONWGSNHA

_____

The U.S. as a World Power 20

Circle the names of three states that entered the Union between 1900 and 1915. (*Hint:* Eliminate states that were in the Revolutionary War or the Civil War.) (Names may continue in the next row.)

GEORGIAOKLAHOMAMAINE

NEWMEXICORHODEISLANDAL

ABAMAARIZONAMISSISSIPPI

The U.S. as a World Power 21

Circle the statement that is true.

World War I started in the United States.

World War I was part of a series of European Wars.

Germany and Great Britain fought on the same side in World War I.

The U.S. as a World Power

The U.S. as a World Power 22

For the first few years of World War I, the United States was neutral. What did that mean?

_____

_____

_____

_____

_____

The U.S. as a World Power 23

Unscramble the kind of ship that sank the passenger liner _Lusitania_ and the kind of weapon it used.

BEURMASIN

_____

ODPTORE

_____

The U.S. as a World Power 24

What is the difference between a merchant vessel and a military vessel?

_____

_____

_____

_____

_____

The U.S. as a World Power 25

Is freedom of the seas as important today as it was in 1917? Why or why not?

_____

_____

_____

_____

_____

_____

The U.S. as a World Power

The U.S. as a World Power 26

Circle all the jobs women did during World War I.

operating computers

working in mills

plowing

nursing

caring for cattle

flying jets

The U.S. as a World Power 27

Who was the Red Baron? Circle the answer.

a Russian general

a British landlord

a German pilot

an American soldier

an Italian pizza maker

The U.S. as a World Power 28

What was another name for World War I? Unscramble the answer.

HET AWR OT DEN LAL SWRA

_____

_____

The U.S. as a World Power 29

Circle the international organization that was formed at the end of World War I. (Names may continue in the next row.)

SECURITYLEAGUEOF

NATIONSNORTHATLA

NTICTREATYORGANI

ZATIONUNITED

NATIONS

The U.S. as a World Power

The U.S. as a World Power 30

Match each general with the war in which he commanded.

Grant   World War II

Washington   Revolutionary War

Eisenhower   World War I

Pershing   Civil War

The U.S. as a World Power 31

On another sheet of paper, write a newspaper article about the 1929 stock market crash.

Facts

Who: investors
What: lost millions of dollars in stock market crash
When: October 24, 1929
Where: New York Stock Exchange
Why: In the booming Twenties, speculators borrowed money to play the market. When they sold overpriced stocks to pay back loans, prices fell.

The U.S. as a World Power 32

It is December 20, 1930. Your father used to own a shoe company. After the stock market crash, nobody could afford new shoes, and his company went out of business. On another sheet of paper, write a diary entry about the difference between your life before the crash and your life now.

STOCK MARKET · DECEMBER 1930

The U.S. as a World Power

The U.S. as a World Power 33

On another sheet of paper, write a newspaper article about the Japanese attack on Pearl Harbor.

Facts

Who: 360 Japanese planes
What: attacked the U.S. Pacific Fleet, sinking eight battleships
Where: Pearl Harbor, Hawaii
When: December 7, 1941
Why: to weaken U.S. power in the Pacific and convince the U.S. to support Japanese expansion in Southeast Asia

The U.S. as a World Power 34

Allies are nations who have agreed to defend each other. Circle nations that were allies of the U.S. in World War II. (Names may continue in the next row.)

JAPANAUSTRALIABRIT

AINITALYCVGERMAN

YTRUSSIAREWQ

CANADASECX

The U.S. as a World Power 35

The allies of Germany in World War II were called the Axis powers. Unscramble the names of two nations that fought on the side of the Axis.

PANAJ

_____

ILAYT

_____

The U.S. as a World Power 36

Number these World War II events in order (1 being the earliest to 5 being the latest).

_____ Japan bombs Pearl Harbor

_____ Germany invades Poland

_____ D-Day invasion of France

_____ U.S. drops hydrogen bomb on Hiroshima, Japan

_____ the Axis occupies France

The U.S. as a World Power

The U.S. as a World Power 37

After World War II, the Soviet Union and the United States fought a long war without firing a shot. Each side made bigger and better bombs and rockets. Each side sent spies to steal the other side's secrets. Unscramble the name of this war.

ETH OLCD AWR

_____

The U.S. as a World Power 38

In 1950, at the request of the United Nations, U.S. forces fought to defend the democratic government of what small Asian nation?

HOSTU REKAO

_____

The U.S. as a World Power 39

Circle the name of a former French colony where U.S. forces fought from 1961–1975.

CANARYISLANDS

CHINAJAPAN

VIETNAMALASKA

NEWZEALAND

The U.S. as a World Power 40

On July 20, 1969, U.S. astronaut Neil Armstrong stepped out onto the surface of the moon. Unscramble his famous quote regarding this *Apollo* moon landing, and write it on the lines below.

"MANKIND LEAP FOR STEP SMALL THAT'S FOR GIANT ONE MAN ONE."

_____

_____

_____

Answer Keys

The Land and First People 1 (p. 2)
Mississippi, Ohio, Missouri, Colorado, Columbia, Rio Grande, Sacramento, Potomac, Hudson, St. Lawrence, Snake, Yukon

The Land and First People 2 (p. 2)
Colorado Plateau

The Land and First People 3 (p. 2)
Florida

The Land and First People 4 (p. 2)
Hawaii

The Land and First People 5 (p. 3)
Appalachian Mountains

The Land and First People 6 (p. 3)
Bering Strait

The Land and First People 7 (p. 3)
Crow, Sioux, Pawnee, Cheyenne, Osage

The Land and First People 8 (p. 3)
Iroquois

The Land and First People 9 (p. 4)
Rocky Mountains, Great Lakes, Great Plains, Atlantic Ocean, Pacific Ocean, Mississippi Delta

The Land and First People 10 (p. 4)
smoke signals

The Land and First People 11 (p. 4)
to communicate with other tribes

The Land and First People 12 (p. 5)
Pueblo, wickiup, tepee, longhouse, hogan, wigwam

The Land and First People 13 (p. 5)
Food, shelter, clothing, fuel

The Land and First People 14 (p. 5)
Because it celebrates the success of European colonization, which was not good for Native Americans

The Land and First People 15 (p. 5)
Seattle, Tecumseh, Cochise, Geronimo, Sitting Bull, Crazy Horse

The Land and First People 16 (p. 6)
Pocahontas, Sacagawea

The Land and First People 17 (p. 6)
mud - pots; grass - baskets; fur - warm robes; deerskin - fringed dresses

The Land and First People 18 (p. 6)
buffalo, deer, seals, bear

The Land and First People 19 (p. 6)
Central Mexico

The Land and First People 20 (p. 7)
arrowheads, spear points, knives

The Land and First People 21 (p. 7)
oak, by rubbing them with smooth rocks

The Land and First People 22 (p. 7)
To fertilize the soil

The Land and First People 23 (p. 7)
Shells, dried fish, seal hides, or any reasonable answer

The Land and First People 24 (p. 8)
Because there was no wood on the plains, and they were always moving to follow the bison

The Land and First People 25 (p. 8)
chestnuts, strawberries, wild rice, fish, turkey

The Land and First People 26 (p. 8)
Native American tribes traded seeds with each other. Native American tribes stored seeds from year to year. Native American women cared for the crops.

The Land and First People 27 (p. 9)
To make beads or any reasonable answer

The Land and First People 28 (p. 9)
sweet potato, corn, squash, tomato, pumpkin

The Land and First People 29 (p. 9)
Native Americans hadn't been exposed to European diseases and had no immunity.

The Land and First People 30 (p. 9)
Cherokee, syllable

The Land and First People 31 (p. 10)
Solutions will vary, but should be symmetrical.

The Land and First People 32 (p. 10)
Alaska

The Land and First People 33 (p. 11)
pots, gourds, sacks or buckets made of animal hide, etc.; rivers, lakes, streams, springs (any two)

The Land and First People 34–36 (p. 11)
Answers will vary.

The Land and First People 37 (p. 12)
Wood homes, hunt bears, warm clothing for winter, fishing, or any other reasonable answers

The Land and First People 38 (p. 12)
Less need for warm clothing in California, reed or mud homes in California, less need to store food for winter, or any other reasonable answers

The Land and First People 39 (p. 12)
More fishing in Florida, fewer plant materials for building in the Southwest, or any other reasonable answers

The Land and First People 40 (p. 12)
Same: play, learn, eat, sleep; Different: live in tepee, learn to hunt or preserve food, ride a horse for transportation, or other reasonable answers

Explorers and Colonizers 1 (p. 13)
Vinland, Leif Ericson, saga

Explorers and Colonizers 2 (p. 13)
salted herring, wool, oil, furs, skins, salt, tar

Explorers and Colonizers 3 (p. 13)
caravel - Portugal; junk - China; dhow - Arabia; canoe - Polynesia; galleon - Spain

Explorers and Colonizers 4 (p. 14)
Polynesians

Explorers and Colonizers 5 (p. 14)
Marco Polo

Explorers and Colonizers 6 (p. 14)
silk, nutmeg, cinnamon, pepper, jewels

Explorers and Colonizers 7 (p. 14)
Find a sea route to India to trade directly, eliminating the middlemen

Explorers and Colonizers 8 (p. 15)
Venice, Genoa, Florence

Explorers and Colonizers 9 (p. 15)
Prince Henry the Navigator, Portugal, Africa

Explorers and Colonizers 10 (p. 15)
astrolabe, quadrant, compass

Explorers and Colonizers 11 (p. 15)
Vasco Da Gama

Explorers and Colonizers 12 (p. 16)
Because Columbus thought he had arrived in the Indies (near India)

Explorers and Colonizers 13 (p. 16)
Bahamas

Explorers and Colonizers 14 (p. 16)
Vasco Nuñez de Balboa

Explorers and Colonizers 15 (p. 16)
Because King Ferdinand and Queen Isabella of Spain paid his expenses

Explorers and Colonizers 16 (p. 17)
Pilgrims - *Mayflower*; Henry Hudson - *Half Moon*; Christopher Columbus - *Santa Maria*

Explorers and Colonizers 17 (p. 17)
Roanoke, Croatoan

Explorers and Colonizers 18 (p. 17)
Jamestown

Explorers and Colonizers 19 (p. 17)
Roger Williams - Rhode Island; William Penn - Pennsylvania; William Bradford - Plymouth Plantation; John Smith - Jamestown

Explorers and Colonizers 20 (p. 18)
Christopher Columbus - a westward route to Asia; Henry Hudson - The Northwest Passage; Juan Ponce de León - The Fountain of Youth; Robert Cavelier de La Salle - Control of the fur trade; William Penn - Tolerance and peace; Hernando Cortéz - Gold and converts

Explorers and Colonizers 21 (p. 18)
Any three of the following: clear the fields, plow to loosen the soil, plant the seeds, pull weeds, harvest the crop, store the crop

Explorers and Colonizers 22 (p. 18)
lobsters, squirrels, rabbits, deer, clams

Explorers and Colonizers 23 (p. 19)
Answers will vary. (current school or classroom news)

Explorers and Colonizers 24 (p. 19)
marbles, corn husk dolls, balls, kites, ice skates

Explorers and Colonizers 25 (p. 19)
spinning wheel

Explorers and Colonizers 26 (p. 19)
loom

Explorers and Colonizers 27 (p. 20)
to teach reading

Explorers and Colonizers 28 (p. 20)
a shared wooden plate

Explorers and Colonizers 29 (p. 20)
smoking, salting, pickling

Explorers and Colonizers 30 (p. 20)
Ships were the only transportation from the Colonies to Europe and from Europe to the Colonies. Without harbors, they would be dashed on the rocks by storms before they could unload.

Explorers and Colonizers 31 (p. 21)
wool - sheep; butter - cow's milk; house - trees; bread - grain; soap - animal fat

Explorers and Colonizers 32 (p. 21)
Because they needed a large, cheap labor force to make their plantations profitable

Explorers and Colonizers 33 (p. 21)
blacksmith - horseshoes; cobbler - shoes; tanner - leather; miller - flour; cooper - barrels

Explorers and Colonizers 34 (p. 22)
maple

Explorers and Colonizers 35 (p. 22)
Sponsors expected colonists to grow, mine, or gather materials needed for manufacturing, and they also expected colonists to buy British manufactured items from them.

Explorers and Colonizers 36 (p. 22)
St. Augustine; Spain

Explorers and Colonizers 37 (p. 22)
Answers will vary. Should include a desire to start a new life in the Colonies.

Explorers and Colonizers 38 (p. 23)
Answers will vary. Experience may be negative or positive.

Explorers and Colonizers 39 (p. 23)
Because Colonial legislatures had not approved the taxes

Explorers and Colonizers 40 (p. 23)
Answers will vary. Should include anger at broken promises and fears that settlers will kill all of the game and take all of the land for themselves.

Revolutionaries and Pioneers 1 (p. 24)
Pennsylvania, New York, North Carolina, New Jersey, South Carolina, Georgia

Revolutionaries and Pioneers 2 (p. 24)
to prevent problems with Native Americans

Revolutionaries and Pioneers 3 (p. 24)
Answers will vary.

Revolutionaries and Pioneers 4 (p. 24)
Daniel Boone

Revolutionaries and Pioneers 5 (p. 25)
Answers will vary.

Revolutionaries and Pioneers 6 (p. 25)
Answers will vary. Finished article should be written in complete sentences and include all the facts.

Revolutionaries and Pioneers 7 (p. 25)
Answers will vary.

Revolutionaries and Pioneers 8 (p. 25)
to seize Patriot supplies

Revolutionaries and Pioneers 9 (p. 26)
Virginia, Massachusetts, Maryland, Rhode Island, Connecticut, Delaware, New Hampshire

Revolutionaries and Pioneers 10 (p. 26)
Henry Wadsworth Longfellow; "Listen my children and you shall hear of the midnight ride of Paul Revere"

Revolutionaries and Pioneers 11 (p. 26)
They were ordinary men who fought on the Patriot side in the Revolutionary War. They pledged to be ready to fight in a minute.

Revolutionaries and Pioneers 12 (p. 27)
Because many generations have learned the poem, and it only speaks of Paul Revere

Revolutionaries and Pioneers 13 (p. 27)
The saying means that you will make more mistakes if you work too fast and, as a result, any job will take longer. An outstanding response will contain a personal example.

Revolutionaries and Pioneers 14 (p. 27)
charm, intelligence, wit

Revolutionaries and Pioneers 15 (p. 27)
13 stars; the 13 original colonies, which became states; 50 stars

Revolutionaries and Pioneers 16 (p. 28)
Yorktown - British surrender;
Philadelphia - Declaration of Independence approved;
Saratoga - Patriot victory in 1777;
Lexington - "The shot heard 'round the world";
Boston - A "tea party";
Valley Forge - A hard winter for Patriots

Revolutionaries and Pioneers 17 (p. 28)
Thomas Jefferson - author of Declaration of Independence;
George Washington - commanded Patriot forces;
Thomas Paine - author of *Common Sense;*
Friedrich von Steuben - trained Patriot troops;
Paul Revere - rode to warn Patriots

Revolutionaries and Pioneers 18 (p. 28)
Margaret Corbin - fought in the war in place of her fallen husband;
Sacagawea - guided Lewis and Clark;
Dolley Madison - saved national treasures from the burning White House
Deborah Sampson - fought in the war disguised as a man
Mercy Otis Warren - wrote political poetry, commentary, and history

Revolutionaries and Pioneers 19 (p. 29)
Answers will vary. May be sad, worried, angry, and/ or proud.

Revolutionaries and Pioneers 20 (p. 29)
1. Boston Massacre; 2. Approval of Declaration of Independence; 3. French fleet arrives; 4. Surrender at Yorktown

Revolutionaries and Pioneers 21 (p. 29)
Fort Ticonderoga

Revolutionaries and Pioneers 22 (p. 29)
Answers will vary.

Revolutionaries and Pioneers 23 (p. 30)
The Battle of Bunker Hill

Revolutionaries and Pioneers 24 (p. 30)
Constitutional Convention

Revolutionaries and Pioneers 25 (p. 30)
Judicial Branch, Executive Branch, Legislative Branch

Revolutionaries and Pioneers 26 (p. 30)
Answers will vary. Might include contempt for the rebels or fears that the ruler's own people might want to form a government without a king or queen

Revolutionaries and Pioneers 27 (p. 31)
To form a more perfect Union; to establish justice
Bonus: to insure domestic tranquility, to provide for the common defense, to promote the general welfare, or to secure the blessings of Liberty to ourselves and our posterity

Revolutionaries and Pioneers 28 (p. 31)
Answers will vary. May name such items as club officers, meeting frequency, or dues

Revolutionaries and Pioneers 29 (p. 31)
The Bill of Rights; Answers will vary.

Revolutionaries and Pioneers 30 (p. 32)
Answers will vary. May include yelling "Fire!" as a joke in a crowded public place or ruining someone's reputation by telling lies.

Revolutionaries and Pioneers 31 (p. 32)
Men who owned land

Revolutionaries and Pioneers 32 (p. 32)
Washington, D.C.; The new states wanted the capital to be on neutral ground so no state would benefit at the expense of the others.

Revolutionaries and Pioneers 33 (p. 32)
The Louisiana Purchase

Revolutionaries and Pioneers 34 (p. 33)
Meriwether Lewis, William Clark

Revolutionaries and Pioneers 35 (p. 33)
steamboat

Revolutionaries and Pioneers 36 (p. 33)
the British; War of 1812

Revolutionaries and Pioneers 37 (p. 34)
Answers will vary, but should use complete sentences and include all information.

Revolutionaries and Pioneers 38–39 (p. 34)
Answers will vary.

Revolutionaries and Pioneers 40 (p. 34)
Advantages: gold dust in miners' clothing, steady work; Disadvantages: prejudice, loneliness, hard work, high prices for necessities

Slavery, Freedom, and Technology 1 (p. 35)
The Pony Express

Slavery, Freedom, and Technology 2 (p. 35)
Morse Code

Slavery, Freedom, and Technology 3 (p. 35)
The Missouri Compromise

Slavery, Freedom, and Technology 4 (p. 35)
The Mason-Dixon Line

Slavery, Freedom, and Technology 5 (p. 36)
Harriet Tubman

Slavery, Freedom, and Technology 6 (p. 36)
removed cotton seeds

Slavery, Freedom, and Technology 7 (p. 36)
More slaves were needed, because more cotton could be processed.

Slavery, Freedom, and Technology 8 (p. 36)
property

Slavery, Freedom, and Technology 9 (p. 37)
When new states came into the Union, it changed the balance of power between the states that allowed slavery and the states that did not.

Slavery, Freedom, and Technology 10 (p. 37)
Answers will vary, but may include: reading makes people think and gives them skills to be independent.

Slavery, Freedom, and Technology 11 (p. 37)
Alabama, Texas, Georgia, Mississippi, Florida, Louisiana

Slavery, Freedom, and Technology 12 (p. 38)
South Carolina

Slavery, Freedom, and Technology 13 (p. 38)
The Confederate States of America

Slavery, Freedom, and Technology 14 (p. 38)
Answers will vary, but might include: the North could make uniforms to keep soldiers warm, dry, and healthy.

Slavery, Freedom, and Technology 15 (p. 38)
The Union wouldn't fight. The Union would give up. England or France would help the South.

Slavery, Freedom, and Technology 16 (p. 39)
Virginia, Arkansas, Tennessee, North Carolina

Slavery, Freedom, and Technology 17 (p. 39)
Fort Sumter

Slavery, Freedom, and Technology 18 (p. 39)
To keep the South from selling crops to raise money and from buying supplies

Slavery, Freedom, and Technology 19 (p. 39)
Gettysburg

Slavery, Freedom, and Technology 20 (p. 40)
Union - Grant, Sherman, Burnside, McClellan;
Confederacy - Lee, Jackson, Longstreet, Beauregard

Slavery, Freedom, and Technology 21 (p. 40)
Appomattox Court House

Slavery, Freedom, and Technology 22 (p. 40)
Emancipation Proclamation; Thirteenth Amendment

Slavery, Freedom, and Technology 23 (p. 41)
Across the continent; transportation, transmission, etc.

Slavery, Freedom, and Technology 24 (p. 41)
To carry people, mail, and supplies to settlements in the West, replacing stagecoaches and covered wagons

Slavery, Freedom, and Technology 25 (p. 41)
Union Pacific - Omaha, west;
Central Pacific - Sacramento, east

Slavery, Freedom, and Technology 26 (p. 41)
grasshoppers

Slavery, Freedom, and Technology 27 (p. 42)
Little House on the Prairie

Slavery, Freedom, and Technology 28 (p. 42)
Advantage: free land, not crowded;
Disadvantage: not enough water, loneliness, insects

Slavery, Freedom, and Technology 29 (p. 42)
Answers will vary.

Slavery, Freedom, and Technology 30 (p. 42)
Plains Tribes: lived in groups, hunted buffalo (bison), lived in tepees;

Homesteaders: lived as single families, lived in sod houses, planted corn

Slavery, Freedom, and Technology 31 (p. 43)
George Armstrong Custer, Little Bighorn,
Chief Sitting Bull

Slavery, Freedom, and Technology 32 (p. 43)
Because people had to know when the train was going to arrive so they could get aboard.

Slavery, Freedom, and Technology 33 (p. 43)
There weren't enough trees to build wood fences. The barbs injured cattle, and cattlemen were used to open range.

Slavery, Freedom, and Technology 34 (p. 44)
Alexander Graham Bell, telephone

Slavery, Freedom, and Technology 35 (p. 44)
phonograph, motion picture machine, light bulb

Slavery, Freedom, and Technology 36 (p. 44)
Answers will vary. Finished article should be written in complete sentences and include all the facts.

Slavery, Freedom, and Technology 37 (p. 44)
Henry Ford, assembly line

Slavery, Freedom, and Technology 38 (p. 45)
Answers will vary.

Slavery, Freedom, and Technology 39 (p. 45)
Wilbur and Orville Wright, airplane

Slavery, Freedom, and Technology 40 (p. 45)
1. Abraham Lincoln elected; 2. Civil War ends;
3. Transcontinental Railroad completed;
4. First successful airplane flight

The U.S. as a World Power 1 (p. 46)
William Astor - real estate; J.P. Morgan - banking;
John D. Rockefeller - oil; Andrew Carnegie - steel

The U.S. as a World Power 2 (p. 46)
strike

The U.S. as a World Power 3 (p. 46)
Eugene Debs, Mother Jones, Samuel Gompers

The U.S. as a World Power 4 (p. 46)
American Federation of Labor

The U.S. as a World Power 5 (p. 47)
Elected representatives and the employer

The U.S. as a World Power 6 (p. 47)
Tenements

The U.S. as a World Power 7 (p. 47)
A fire; Drawing should be of a cow.

The U.S. as a World Power 8 (p. 48)
Answers will vary.

The U.S. as a World Power 9 (p. 48)
Booker T. Washington

The U.S. as a World Power 10 (p. 48)
Answers will vary. Might include the idea that immigrants want to keep their own distinct cultures.

The U.S. as a World Power 11 (p. 48)
Answers will vary. May include the fact that if there is competition, customers will buy from those who offer the best products or services at the best prices.

The U.S. as a World Power 12 (p. 49)
Maine; It exploded and sank in Havana's harbor.

The U.S. as a World Power 13 (p. 49)
newspaper articles (Hearst papers)

The U.S. as a World Power 14 (p. 49)
Philippine Islands, Guam, Puerto Rico

The U.S. as a World Power 15 (p. 50)
Rough Riders

The U.S. as a World Power 16 (p. 50)
He was vice president when the president was shot.

The U.S. as a World Power 17 (p. 50)
Theodore Roosevelt - Trust-busting;
William McKinley - Spanish-American War;
Herbert Hoover - The Great Depression;
Woodrow Wilson - World War I

The U.S. as a World Power 18 (p. 51)
1. Abraham Lincoln, 2. Theodore Roosevelt,
3. Woodrow Wilson, 4. John F. Kennedy

The U.S. as a World Power 19 (p. 51)
North Dakota, Montana, South Dakota, Washington

The U.S. as a World Power 20 (p. 51)
Oklahoma, New Mexico, Arizona

The U.S. as a World Power 21 (p. 51)
World War I was part of a series of European Wars.

The U.S. as a World Power 22 (p. 52)
The United States was not fighting on either side.

The U.S. as a World Power 23 (p. 52)
submarine, torpedo

The U.S. as a World Power 24 (p. 52)
A merchant vessel carries passengers or freight, but a military vessel is designed for fighting.

The U.S. as a World Power 25 (p. 52)
Though still very important, it is not as crucial now because most passengers and many goods are carried by air.

The U.S. as a World Power 26 (p. 53)
working in mills, plowing, nursing, caring for cattle

The U.S. as a World Power 27 (p. 53)
a German pilot

The U.S. as a World Power 28 (p. 53)
The War to End All Wars

The U.S. as a World Power 29 (p. 53)
League of Nations

The U.S. as a World Power 30 (p. 54)
Grant - Civil War; Washington - Revolutionary War; Eisenhower - World War II; Pershing - World War I

The U.S. as a World Power 31 (p. 54)
Answers will vary. Should be written in complete sentences and include all facts.

The U.S. as a World Power 32 (p. 54)
Answers will vary. Might include loss of home and possessions.

The U.S. as a World Power 33 (p. 55)
Answers will vary. Should be written in complete sentences and include all facts.

The U.S. as a World Power 34 (p. 55)
Australia, Britain, Russia, Canada

The U.S. as a World Power 35 (p. 55)
Japan, Italy

The U.S. as a World Power 36 (p. 55)
1. Germany invades Poland
2. The Axis occupies France
3. Japan bombs Pearl Harbor
4. D-Day invasion of France
5. U.S. drops hydrogen bomb on Hiroshima, Japan

The U.S. as a World Power 37 (p. 56)
The Cold War

The U.S. as a World Power 38 (p. 56)
South Korea

The U.S. as a World Power 39 (p. 56)
Vietnam

The U.S. as a World Power 40 (p. 56)
"That's one small step for man, one giant leap for mankind."